Speaking Life To The Nation!

(United States Of America)

Declarations to Speak Out Loud for Your Nation And Community

By Joel Yount

Speaking Life to the Nation

Copyright © 2022 Joel Yount

All rights reserved.

All Rights Reserved. No part of this publication may be reproduced, stored in a retrieval system or transmitted in any form or by any means – online, electronic, mechanical, photocopy, recording or any other – except for brief quotations in printed reviews, without prior permission of the author.

For the word of God is alive and active. Sharper than any double-edged sword, it penetrates even to dividing soul and spirit, joints and marrow; it judges the thoughts and attitudes of the heart. **(Hebrews 4:12)**

"Just like Shadrach, Meshach, and Abednego, God will be with you in your fiery furnace trials of life. Remain strong and refuse to back down. Your survival could IMPACT future generations for the Kingdom of God! Move forward TODAY in the plans and dreams God has been speaking to you. Place all fears on trial. Advancement is Coming!"

--Joel Yount

Table of Contents

Introduction 11

Powerful Scriptures *I Like to Declare Daily in My Prayer Life*... 13

Speaking Words *Of Life Into Your Family*..17

Prayer *for High Profile Public Figures & Celebrities* 21

Speaking Words *of Life Against the Evil Work of Human Traffickers*.......................... 23

Speaking Life *Over the News Media* 27

Speaking Life *into Your Local City Government*.. 31

Speaking Life *Over Your Local Schools* 37

Speaking Life *into Your Neighborhood* 41

Prayer *for Transportation in My Nation* 45

Declaring Divine Protection *& Assistance from Angels Over the Nation's Borders* 47

Prayer *for Protection Over the Nation's Capital, the White House, the President, & Those in Congress* 51

A Breakthrough *for Intercessors: A Bridge Between Law Enforcement and Prayer Warriors!* 55

Section 2: *Encouragement for Your Journey Ahead* 59

From Confinement to Freedom *Declaring The Wall Of Resistance to Move!* 61

Rest in the Rain 65

Who Is Looking Out for You? 71

Feeling Discouraged *and Ready To Quit?*
This Is a Word For Someone Today! 75

Introduction

One thing I have learned recently is the power in decreeing and declaring scripture out loud. For years, I cannot remember speaking verbal prayer and declaration which is completely opposite to the way I am now. As I continue to speak the word of God out loud daily, I am seeing my spirit man strengthened and built up. I am seeing situations turn around! As believers in the body of Christ we need to be equipped with a strategy to speak life--not just in our own being but for the bigger community we live in. I believe God has laid it upon my heart to create a resource that would be a springboard for people to begin praying out loud and declaring life to the nation. As we recognize and move forward more into the power of prayer, get ready for shifts to occur that will radically impact the nation! As sons and daughters in the Kingdom, get ready to use your authority to call forth Life into the impossible!

SPEAKING LIFE TO THE NATION!

Powerful Scriptures
I Like to Declare Daily in My Prayer Life

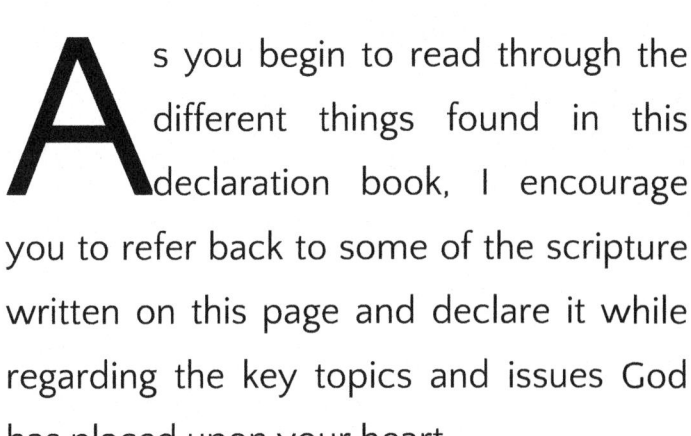

As you begin to read through the different things found in this declaration book, I encourage you to refer back to some of the scripture written on this page and declare it while regarding the key topics and issues God has placed upon your heart.

Psalm 12:5

"Because the poor are plundered and the needy groan, I will now arise," says the Lord. "I will protect them from those who malign them."

Isaiah 54:17

No weapon forged against you will prevail, and you will refute every tongue that accuses you.

This is the heritage of the servants of the Lord, and this is their vindication from me," declares the Lord.

SPEAKING LIFE TO THE NATION!

Philippians 4:19

And my God will meet all your needs according to the riches of his glory in Christ Jesus.

Isaiah 40:31

but those who hope in the Lord will renew their strength. They will soar on wings like eagles; they will run and not grow weary, they will walk and not be faint.

Psalm 90:17

May the favor[a] of the Lord our God rest on us; establish the work of our hands for us— yes, establish the work of our hands.

Hebrews 4:12

For the word of God is alive and active. Sharper than any double-edged sword, it penetrates even to dividing soul and spirit, joints and marrow; it judges the thoughts and attitudes of the heart.

Speaking Words *Of Life Into Your Family*

——★ ★ ★——

Heavenly Father, I come before you today and stand in agreement for unity in my family. In Jesus's name I decree life, clarity, and peace to flow like a river into my family and extended family members. I call forth your love to infiltrate even the family members that easily irritate me or get on my nerves.

Show them your love God so love will begin to pour out of them.

Right now, I come into agreement and speak life into every member of my family for wisdom, protection, and healing with their emotions. I call forth your angels to be dispatched according to your will in heaven to stand guard and protect my family. Every plot or attack of the enemy that is being planned behind the scenes I decree it be foiled in Jesus's name.

Thank you God, as I am calling forth life and destiny into my children's future. Thank you Lord, for Godly and healthily influential people will come alongside them to form a positive culture for them to grow up in.

SPEAKING LIFE TO THE NATION!

Prayer
for High Profile Public Figures & Celebrities

Heavenly Father, we come into agreement right now for those in the public eye that hold celebrity status or are in powerful positions. We call forth peace and rest to fill the hearts of celebrities with your love and desires. Lord, give your eyes to people to see celebrities and people in high profile public figure status the way you see them. Helps us to see them through eyes of grace and compassion so we can more effectively pray for them. We call forth favor into those in Hollywood for opportunities to further advance your Kingdom in the days ahead!

Speaking Words
of Life Against the Evil Work of Human Traffickers

Heavenly Father, we approach you today on the topic of human trafficking. Lord, send forth your warrior angels and light to uncover and reveal any human trafficking rings in my local area and to have them brought to justice and understanding. I pray that truth would be revealed and that light would expose any darkness that is associated with this atrocity.

In Jesus's name I declare Isaiah 54:17 over my city and local community. I pray that wisdom would be given to local law enforcement to effectively dismantle the evil work of human traffickers.

No weapon forged against you will prevail, and you will refute every tongue that accuses you. This is the heritage of the servants of the Lord, and this is their vindication from me," declares the Lord.

(Isaiah 54:17)

SPEAKING LIFE TO THE NATION!

Thank you Lord for your protection and the angelic assistance for my city!

Speaking Life
Over the News Media

———★ ★ ★———

Heavenly Father, we thank You for the impact that good news brings. I come into agreement right now for the local media in my area to report accurate and truthful news stories. I pray for righteousness to arise from Your Spirit to fill the local media airwaves in my area. I pray that you establish and deploy reporters and news anchors of integrity into my region to fulfill your purposes.

In Jesus's name I come into agreement now for the national media in my country to be infiltrated with righteousness and truth. I decree and declare life to arise within the airwaves on cable and network news outlets for your glory. Anything that may be hindering or holding back truth that needs to be sent forth we speak release now in Jesus's name! We call forth the release of truth, honesty, and integrity over the media landscape right now. For the future of my city, state, and nation, Lord we call forth the mountain of news media to begin to align greater with your Kingdom plans and purposes in this hour.

Speaking Life
into Your Local City Government

———★ ★ ★———

1. Heavenly Father, I come before You right now and I am choosing to speak life to my local city government. I speak life, health, and prosperity to those living in my city. I call forth favor for new development for housing, new businesses, and families to all flourish. We speak creativity over local

developers and call them into my local area to initiate plans that are in Heaven to begin to be created in the natural here in my city.

2. I call forth life into local decision making that will have a positive impact in my city. Any plan by any individual that would attempt to create a delay or stalling of any project that would hinder the growth and development of my city we say no way! Lord, have your way! We call forth Your resurrection power to resurrect the blueprints you have in heaven for my city in Jesus's name. Let your heavenly blueprints flow and resonate within the hearts of every

member of my local city council and government departments. I pray that every member of my local city council has a radical encounter with your love that flows through them from their head to their toes. We pray for divine protection for every member of my local city council and call forth your angels to assist in protecting them. Any piece of legislation or proposal that would attempt to be presented to my local city council that is not of you Lord or Your will we speak and call forth a divine stop to its progression.

3. Heavenly Father, I call forth Your watchmen and intercessors to be established within my city. I thank You, our Lord, for speaking to us in dreams and visions so that we can alert those around us of plans of the enemy. I thank You, Heavenly Father, that I have the ability to receive advance warnings and alerts regarding any violent attacks planned in my city. We call forth divine favor for intercessors and watchmen to make strong connections with my local city council and mayor and local authorities.

Romans 12:2

Do not conform to the pattern of this world, but be transformed by the renewing of your mind. Then you will be able to test and approve what God's will is—his good, pleasing and perfect will.

Psalm 121:7-8

The Lord will keep you from all harm—he will watch over your life; **8** the Lord will watch over your coming and going both now and forevermore.

Speaking Life
Over Your Local Schools
———★ ★ ★———

Heavenly Father, I thank You for the schools local to my area. Right now, I choose to decree and declare rivers of life into every student, teacher, and staff member that are involved in the education system. I call forth a powerful revelation of your love to overflow each of them so that they would begin to impart Your love and wisdom onto the students.

Today, I am choosing to call forth the angels to be sent forth according to Your will God to bring forth and establish protection for every student and staff member in my local school system.

Heavenly Father, any and all needs that my local school system has in need of we ask that you grant your favor for provision for the needs to be met so that the children in my area receive the best education possible.

Last but not least, Lord, we ask that your presence would flow through each school in my local area that would impact future generations for your Kingdom. We call forth light and life into this very important mission field of our education system. Amen.

Speaking Life
into Your Neighborhood

——★ ★ ★——

1. Heavenly Father, I decree and declare life into the atmosphere of my neighborhood. I ask that Your Heavenly peace to flow like a river into homes and apartments on my street right now. I pray for the revelation of Your love to be poured out in every family that lives in my area. I thank You for the signs and

confirmation that will flow into their lives in the coming days and weeks ahead that reveal your Love to them in ways only You can do.

2. I pray and declare life on every street corner and hidden area of my neighborhood. I pray You would reveal every plot of the enemy that would seek to destroy the future of anyone in my neighborhood. We call forth Your angels to assist and help combat any attack the enemy may be planning right now to take territory in my neighborhood. We thank You God that your power and authority is greater than the enemy.

3. In Jesus's name we speak life to the children in my neighborhood and we call forth your protection from any influences that would seek to devour their spiritual walk with you Lord. We call forth Godly influences in their life and for your angels of protection to create and mighty fortress ushering them into learning Godly moral values that will preserve them for their future.

Isaiah 55:11

so is my word that goes out from my mouth: It will not return to me empty, but will accomplish what I desire and achieve the purpose for which I sent it.

Proverbs 18:21

The tongue has the power of life and death, and those who love it will eat its fruit.

Prayer
for Transportation in My Nation

Heavenly Father, I lift up my nation's transportation system right now. I pray for a hedge of protection around vehicles of transportation, airplanes, and other avenues of transit. I pray that your angels of protection are sent forth to roadways and interstates around my nation to disrupt plans of the enemy.

In Jesus's name we decree that individuals who are planning evil and harm to my nation will be overtaken by the radical love of God and will have a heart change. We call forth individuals from the enemy's camp to be radically changed and turned into powerful evangelists for the Kingdom of God!

Isaiah 54:17

no weapon forged against you will prevail, and you will refute every tongue that accuses you. This is the heritage of the servants of the Lord, and this is their vindication from me," declares the Lord.

SPEAKING LIFE TO THE NATION!

Declaring Divine Protection

& Assistance from Angels Over the Nation's Borders

———★ ★ ★———

Heavenly Father, we come into agreement today and call forth your divine protection over the nation's borders. Any individual or groups of people that may be planning attacks or strategies against the nation we call forth a divine halt in their tracks from moving forward and toward darkness. We decree and declare divine interceptions in the realm of the spirit to put a stop to the plans of the enemy regarding intrusion at the borders of the nation. In Jesus's name we invite Your angels and pray according to your will in heaven to release your angel armies to set up camp around every border, every hidden place, and every hidden tunnel that the enemy thinks is hidden from plain view. We also pray for uncovering and revealing those who are trusted to protect the nation's borders but are actually associated with outside plans of enemies of the nation. Lord, have your way and we call forth alignment into who is supposed to be guarding the borders and a release of those who are not fulfilling this important task. We even call forth favor for honest security guards at the nation's border right now in Jesus's mighty name!

SPEAKING LIFE TO THE NATION!

Prayer

for Protection Over the Nation's Capital, the White House, the President, & Those in Congress

——★★★——

Heavenly Father, we come before you right now and declare Your wisdom into those in authority at the Nation's capital. We pray the issues that are pressing on Your heart begin to manifest at an accelerated rate. In Jesus's name we call forth favor for dreams and visions during the night for members of congress and the President & Vice President. Lord, show each individual in authority over the nation Your heart into key issues regarding the nation. Surround them Lord with Godly influences that will speak into their life and build a reservoir of waters of life in the spirit that will cause them to grow in the things of the spirit. What the enemy meant for harm, we call forth a backfire in the spirit for restoration that will multiply the impact for God's Kingdom in every hallway and meeting room of Congress in Jesus's name!

SPEAKING LIFE TO THE NATION!

Every building, every monument, and every national landmark that may try to become a target of attack from the camp of the enemy we pray that your divine protection and angels be released to set up camp around those areas today. Lord, cover us with the blood of Jesus and keep us safe from the distractions and plots of the enemy.

In Jesus's name, we call forth by faith that the United States will be known as a nation that stands for life! We pray boldness into every politician to begin to arise greater than ever before to stand for laws that bring forth righteousness and life to the nation.

SPEAKING LIFE TO THE NATION!

A Breakthrough
for Intercessors: A Bridge Between Law Enforcement and Prayer Warriors!

———★ ★ ★———

I believe God is connecting prayer warriors in cities across the United States and around the world at an accelerated rate!

A few weeks ago, I felt led to begin to pray for law enforcement and prayer intercessors for a great bridge of unity between the two groups. In the days to come, I believe a strong connection between these two groups are going to help be the catalyst for a level of breakthrough and answered prayers for the nation and around the world!

I can see a group of intercessors taking notes on paper and then communicating with law enforcement and intelligence officials regarding tips they've received in dreams and visions. These heavenly communications delivered by the intercessors were then used to help intelligence and law enforcement officials to narrow their focus and take down plans of the enemy with accuracy! I see this happening not just in a few small groups but with the potential to grow in every city across the globe!

I am thankful for those that have the seer gift. Heavenly Father, protect those that are seeing things in advance to alert us to pray!

Prayer Point: Let's lift up law enforcement and intelligence officials in prayer that there would be favor between them and prophetic voices to work together to interrupt plans of the enemy.

Section 2:
Encouragement for Your Journey Ahead

SPEAKING LIFE TO THE NATION!

From Confinement to Freedom
Declaring The Wall Of Resistance to Move!

I'll never forget years ago a movie I watched where a young mother and her small child were trapped and confined to a small room. There seemed to be no way out. I thought to myself, one of these days are they going to plan an escape? I can't imagine the level of fear the woman had knowing that the individual keeping her and her son locked away in a small area might do if she wasn't successful in her attempt to run away and get help.

You see this woman and child weren't just facing isolation, but they were also facing resistance from getting free. It's one thing to want to escape and be free but another thing to battle the fear and anxiety if whoever is holding them catches them in their attempt to run away.

I believe many of us in recent months especially have faced different levels of resistance. Resistance from moving forward, launching new blueprints, and projects. When it feels like a wall of resistance is in front of us from advancing it often makes us want to give up.

Several months ago, I felt like giving up on something new I started. It would be easier to just quit right than to push past the difficulties? Later that evening I got a message from someone saying, "The Lord wants to encourage you. Keep Going. You Are a Warrior! There Is a Reward Coming." That short dose of encouragement was the fuel I needed to not want to give up. I kept going and now going full speed ahead!

Today, let me encourage you... don't give up! You are a warrior and backing out now is not in your DNA. The Wall of Resistance trying to stand in front of you must come down in Jesus's name! I speak to that wall right now and tell it to begin to crumble in all directions. The warrior heart God placed in you is no match for the obstacles in front of you. That's the breaking news that the enemy doesn't want you to hear right now.

Begin to declare out loud that your Wall of Resistance is coming down!

Rest in the Rain

—★ ★ ★—

The other day while listening to the sound of the rain, I felt a peace begin to come upon me. The rain hitting against the wooden porch was just so soothing. When some people think of rain, they might describe it as gloomy or think of it as just another rainy day. I have found though when I listen in closer to the big drops falling from the sky onto the ground there's something more to be heard. As I quieted my spirit before the Lord, I began to feel His peace, His presence, and His love overwhelming my heart. It was then I realized I wasn't complaining about another rainy day but was thankful about entering into a day of rest. Rest for my soul, spirit, and body.

Allowing God's love to fill every fiber of our being so we are transformed into sons and daughters who bring light into the world when we are now needed most. It's a time where God is going after roots. Many are wondering why the anchors of fear and anger seek to reign over nations. Perhaps it is what we allow to take root in our hearts by what we listen to and the emotions that are birthed as a result. In the midst of confusion and chaos, God tells us to not fear.

"Fear not, for I am with you; be not dismayed, for I am your God; I will strengthen you, I will help you, I will uphold you with my righteous right hand"
– (Isaiah 41:10 ESV.)

My friend, you are a treasure. Though you may feel broken or bruised, your heavenly Father sees you as a treasure that maybe the rest of the world hasn't fully seen just yet. Through the pain and heartache that has hit many in recent years rain may not always be the most joyful thing to remember. Perhaps it might remind people of the many tears they have shed over loved ones that have passed.

However, I believe a deep construction of hearts is being orchestrated right now where God is ushering in a love that will flow out into the world and begin to fill those places where the pain has been too much to take because of loss. For those of you who have gotten used to shedding tears, I want to encourage you with hope. Let your heavenly Father's love capture you with the fragrance of his heart. He wants you to rest and be still. For there are fresh words of comfort He has to speak to you that will help enter you into a restful season of victory!

"He says, 'Be still, and know that I am God; I will be exalted among the nations, I will be exalted in the earth'"

(Psalm 46:10 NIV)

In the coming days or weeks ahead as you begin to listen to the sound of rain more closely, just remember a season of rest is here for you. It's time to feel rest in the rain and in the comfort of the Father's embrace.

SPEAKING LIFE TO THE NATION!

Who Is Looking Out for You?

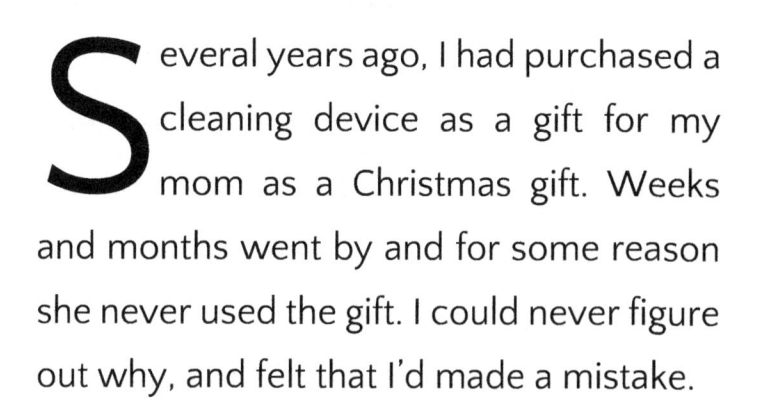

—★ ★ ★—

Several years ago, I had purchased a cleaning device as a gift for my mom as a Christmas gift. Weeks and months went by and for some reason she never used the gift. I could never figure out why, and felt that I'd made a mistake.

As time went on, I kept asking, "Mom, did you use that new cleaning device that I got you as a gift?" She would tell me that she didn't have time to use it yet.

A few months ago, I received a letter in the mail that notified me of an important product recall on this very same cleaning device that I purchased as the gift for my mom. The letter contained details of some alarming things that have happened to some people who used this machine. I was absolutely stunned. It all of a sudden hit me that maybe my mom was being protected by not using it after all. Maybe it was the hand of the Lord who cautioned her to not use it yet.

SPEAKING LIFE TO THE NATION!

Friends, in life we do not always understand why we feel like there may be some delay or we feel puzzled as to why something is not happening yet but God knew the future ahead of time about this specific gift I had gotten way back and the news that would be released about it later down the road. God is good and He was protecting my mom the whole time.

So thankful our heavenly Father is looking out for us!

Feeling Discouraged
and Ready To Quit? This Is a Word For Someone Today!

———★ ★ ★———

You may have had numerous prophetic words spoken over you regarding acceleration in your life... but may have not seen any doors open yet.

This is a word for someone today!

Flowers are beginning to spring up from the ground in your life. The tears you have shed in the past have not been wasted. It's not over until God says it's over! Keep climbing up the MOUNTAIN. Your persistence is leading to your breakthrough!

Just like Shadrach, Meshach, and Abednego, God will be with you in your fiery furnace trials of life. Remain strong and refuse to back down. Your survival could IMPACT future generations for the Kingdom of God! Move forward TODAY in the plans and dreams God has been speaking to you. Place all fears on trial.

Advancement is Coming!

"I am the LORD, the God of all mankind. Is anything too hard for me?" – (Jeremiah 32:27.)

God is bringing you through the tests to create your testimony!

The strong winds of adversity attempting to blow you down are moving you into NEW blessings and territory!

Dear Reader,

If your life was touched while reading "Speaking Life to the Nation" please let us know! We would love to celebrate with you! Please email me at. joel.yount@yahoo.com

Blessings,
Joel Yount

Joel Yount's passion is helping to advance the Kingdom of God with encouragement. Encourager, Writer, and Speaker

Joel Yount

Encouragement for Now, LLC.

P.O. Box 2134

Lake City, FL 32055

Email

Joel@EncouragementForNow.com

Ministry links

https://linktr.ee/joelyount

EncouragementForNow.com

Ministry and Speaking Engagements

If you are interested in having Joel minister or speak at your church, gathering or event, please contact him at

Joel@encouragementfornow.com

Made in the USA
Middletown, DE
15 March 2022